T0120982

Evaluation

of the

Positive Behavior Support Program

on

Fourth-Grade Student Discipline Infractions

DR. JAMES A. BRACY

authorHOUSE®

AuthorHouse™
1663 Liberty Drive
Bloomington, IN 47403
www.authorhouse.com
Phone: 1 (800) 839-8640

© 2018 DR. JAMES A. BRACY. All rights reserved.

No part of this book may be reproduced, stored in a retrieval system, or transmitted by any means without the written permission of the author.

Published by AuthorHouse 02/26/2018

ISBN: 978-1-5462-2883-7 (sc)
ISBN: 978-1-5462-2882-0 (e)

Library of Congress Control Number: 2018901903

Print information available on the last page.

Any people depicted in stock imagery provided by Thinkstock are models, and such images are being used for illustrative purposes only. Certain stock imagery © Thinkstock.

This book is printed on acid-free paper.

Because of the dynamic nature of the Internet, any web addresses or links contained in this book may have changed since publication and may no longer be valid. The views expressed in this work are solely those of the author and do not necessarily reflect the views of the publisher, and the publisher hereby disclaims any responsibility for them.

Acknowledgments

First and most important, I would like to thank God who has been able to bring me this far. I would also like to thank each of those who contributed to me finishing this process: Dr. Marcia O'Brien who has guided me though endless papers and corrections; Dr. Eugene Costa who helped guide me through my class selection; and my cohort members Phyllis Gordon and Cynthia Evans who have called, e-mailed, and kept in touch to make sure that I was staying on track.

Last, but not least, I thank my family for all of their support, patience, love, and understanding. To my wife, Eleanor, I know that it has not been easy to deal with all of the time spent on school work and sleepless nights, but you always stood right beside me. You are the best wife I could ever ask for. To my daughter, Erica, Daddy is proud of you and really appreciated all of your help. To my daughter, April, after countless nights of typing and retyping papers, we have finally made it. The journey is over, and it is now time to sit back and enjoy the benefits of all the hard work. I love you all.

ABSTRACT

Evaluation of the Positive Behavior Support Program on Fourth-Grade Student Discipline Infractions. James A. Bracy, 2010: Applied Dissertation, Nova Southeastern University, Fischler School of Education and Human Services. ERIC Descriptors: Student Behavior, Program Evaluation, Antisocial Behavior, Program Effectiveness.

Students with increased antisocial behaviors are becoming more disruptive to the learning environment on a regular basis. Because much of the instructional time is being spent correcting these behaviors, the academic progression of students has been decreasing. To limit distractions, disruptive students need to be remediated and counseled on problems and solutions. The Positive Behavior Support (PBS) program is an alternative to giving students negative attention by rewarding them for good behavior and teaching them that good choices breed good consequences.

The purpose of the study was to examine the implementation of a PBS program and its effectiveness in diminishing undesirable behaviors. Results showed that the PBS program did diminish the behavior based on the number of referrals received in the preintervention school year and the postintervention school year. Nevertheless, some teachers and parents believed that the PBS program could be improved for total effectiveness of the program.

Surveys on the PBS program were administered to parents, students, and staff. Seventy- two percent of parents indicated that the PBS program was an effective means of curbing the number of student code of conduct violations although 60% of all the parents thought that it could be more effective if there were some changes made to the program. Seventy-one percent of the students liked the program, but, just as the parents, 35% of them believed that there were some changes that needed to be made. As for the faculty of the target school, 60% believed that the program was effective, but 85% believed that some changes needed to be made. All the stakeholders agreed that, overall, the program was effective in curbing student code of conduct violations, but, with a few simple changes, it could be much more effective.

Implications for future research were discussed. More studies should be conducted for students with deeply rooted societal problems and for exceptional learners who have a greater need for counseling.

CONTENTS

CHAPTER 1

Introduction

Nature and Significance of the Problem

At the end of the 2003-2004 school year, school district officials collected data that indicated a high number of student suspensions in Grades 4 through 6. A closer look at these data showed that many of the same students were suspended repeatedly. During this school year, there were 43 out-of-school suspensions in the study school (School A), but only 30 students were suspended. Also, it is important to note that, during this school year, there were 525 students enrolled; therefore, on average, about 6% of the students were suspended at some point. This means that many of the students who were suspended during the 2003-2004 school year were suspended on more than one occasion. These students were obviously having problems with exhibiting or maintaining appropriate behaviors (Delaware Department of Education, 2008).

There were four other elementary schools in the study site school district (Schools B, C, D, and E). The students at each of these schools were also exhibiting problems with student code of conduct infractions.

For instance, there were a total number of 974 students enrolled at School B in the 2003-2004 school year. There were 76 suspensions that year, but only 44 students were suspended. This averages to about 4.5% of the student population being suspended. This problem seemed to be occurring at School C more than any other school. There were only 240 students enrolled, but there were 43 suspensions and 32 students suspended. This means that 13% of the student population was suspended that school year. School D's profile was very similar to School A's profile. There were 972 students enrolled, 44 suspensions, and 28 students suspended from School D. On average, about 3% of the

1

student population was suspended from school at some point. School E seemed to be the only intermediate school in the school district that was not having a significant problem with student suspensions. There were 380 students enrolled in the 2003-2004 school year, but only two suspensions by two different students. This means that only 0.5% of the student population at this school was suspended (Delaware Department of Education, 2008).

In the spring of 2004, after this information was released to the staff of School A, the teachers, administrators, and counselors began discussing their concerns that the students at this elementary school were not complying with code of conduct rules. Most staff members predicted that the problem was only going to get worse if some type of intervention was not implemented. The school guidance counselor learned that most of the suspensions were due to offensive touching and aggressive response to stimuli. She suggested that school personnel consider implementing an anger management program.

During the summer after the 2003-2004 school year, a planning team of administrators and the school guidance counselor examined and researched several anger management programs and shared their findings with the entire faculty and staff. Once the Stop and Think Social Skills Intervention program was decided upon, the guidance counselor and administrators worked around the clock to develop and design a plan for the intervention program, including a mission statement and goals (Todd, Kauffman, Meyer, & Horner, 2008).

During the 2004-2005 school year, only 14 students were reportedly suspended from School A (see Table 1), but this soon changed. During the 2005-2006 school year, in School A, 92 student code of conduct infractions were committed, resulting in 92 suspensions. This was obviously the highest number of suspensions that the administration at this school had seen in a long time (see Table 2).

Table 1

Suspension Data for the 2004-2005 School Year

Category	School A	School B	School C	School D	School E
No. of students	544	1,029	228	915	344
No. of suspensions	14	220	5	6	11
No. of students suspended	14	180	5	4	6
% of students suspended	3	10	2	1	2

It was clear from the recent research that the suspension rate at School A was still high. In the 2006-2007 school year, there were 440 students enrolled at the school of whom 37 students (8%) were suspended (see Table 3). This number increased in the 2007-2008 school year. During this school year, there were only 388 students enrolled of whom 90 students (23%) were suspended (Delaware Department of Education, 2008).

As a fourth-grade teacher who has been employed with the school district for more than 14 years, this researcher was able to experience firsthand the problems associated with student discipline. Faculty and staff members had high hopes that the first behavioral intervention program, the Stop and Think Social Skills Intervention program (as cited in Todd et al., 2008) that was implemented in the 2004-2005 school year, would have a significant impact on this high number, but this simply was not the case.

In fact, the number of the suspensions and the percentage of students being suspended had actually risen (see Tables 1 and 2). The high number of suspensions was having a negative impact on the teachers and students. For instance, students who did not have behavioral problems were becoming frustrated with the constant disruption of their learning process. Teachers were becoming more and more discouraged and were losing hope for a change.

Table 2

Suspension Data for the 2005-2006 School Year

Category	School A	School B	School C	School D	School E
No. of students	415	863	256	1,185	312
No. of suspensions	92	129	156	219	103
No. of students suspended	51	90	71	115	71
% of students suspended	12	10	28	10	23

To combat this problem, school personnel continued to look for another behavioral prevention program that would be more effective. The staff spent time studying the Positive Behavior Support (PBS) program (Carr et al., 2002) and found that it had been effective in other public schools around the nation. Therefore, in October of 2007, personnel at School A decided to implement the PBS program.

Also, during the summer of 2008, school district officials at the target school restructured the intermediate schools to make them all elementary schools. Previously, students from Grades 4 to 6 attended intermediate schools, but, currently, the elementary schools service students in kindergarten-Grade 5, and students in the sixth grade are now bused to the middle schools.

Table 3

Suspension Data for the 2006-2007 School Year

Category	School A	School B	School C	School D	School E
No. of students	440	854	248	1,126	312
No. of suspensions	42	132	159	203	107
No. of students suspended	37	92	76	109	72
% of students suspended	8	11	31	10	23

Purpose of the Study

Personnel in the target school implemented the PBS program because of the high suspension rate (12% of the students suspended during the 2005-2006 school year; see Table 2). It was evident that the Stop and Think Social Skills Intervention program was not effective in reducing the number of suspensions. Therefore, the PBS program was implemented in the 2006-2007 school year. This study was designed to determine if the PBS program was, indeed, effective at reducing the number of student code of conduct infractions at this urban intermediate school. In addition, this researcher helped identify those elements of the program that were effective and areas that were in need of improvement. The researcher examined participants', teachers', and parents' opinions and ideas about this program as well as the number of suspensions.

The study was open to all teachers who participated in the program to give their input. There were 34 teachers involved in the study. As a teacher in School A, the researcher had also actively participated in this program and had firsthand knowledge of how it was supposed to be implemented as well as some of the pros and cons of the program.

Background and Significance of the Study

A top priority for educators in the United States is to understand and prevent inappropriate behavior in schools by American youth. Two different approaches have been developed in the United States in an attempt to combat this problem. In-school and out-of-school suspensions, coupled with parent notification and possible legal action, represent one approach. This approach is aimed at reducing the number of student code of conduct violations by means of punishment for the offenses. The second approach relies on intervention and education concerning the negative aspects of inappropriate behavior. Neither approach has proved 100% effective in addressing this problem. Research and evaluation of school intervention programs are necessary to determine if these programs are actually helping to solve the problem. The study site is an urban intermediate school that has students enrolled from Grades 4 to 6 and is situated in the center of

Delaware's largest city. This school is fairly young compared to other schools in the city and has been in operation for over 50 years, dating back to 1958. School enrollment is 440 students, and the student: teacher ratio is 15:1.

Of 440 students in this school, 60% are minorities, and 57% come from low- income families. It is also important to note that 1% of the students use English as a second language and 17% receive special education services. Only 31% of the faculty is minority, and 35% has less than 3 years of teaching experience.

All students at School A are required to follow the school district's code of conduct. A copy of the code of conduct handbook is made available to all parents and students at the beginning of the school year. Throughout the year, students are held accountable for any violation through appropriate consequences. An in-school suspension program has been established, and incentives such as field trips, parties, and extra recess time are offered to those students who exhibit good behavior and effort.

During the 2004-2005 school year, the staff implemented the Stop and Think Social Skills Intervention program. The teaching staff stated that implementing this program did not help combat the problem. To help avoid any further code of conduct violations, the PBS program was implemented at School A since October 2007. States such as Iowa, Florida, and Delaware use the PBS program. The Delaware Department of Education (2008) started the initiative 10 years ago and invited school district officials to train teams to start implementing the process. The school district in which School A is located was one of the first school districts to implement the PBS program; however, the administration at School A did not implement this program until October 2007.

All students participated in this program, which was implemented in all areas of the school by teachers and school staff. With a foundation in traditional behavioral sciences, the PBS program has grown to enhance all-inclusive interventions for individuals with disabilities (Carr et al., 2002). Recently, employment of the PBS program approach has included various locations, students who receive special education services, and an expansive reach of inappropriate behaviors. Therefore, the PBS program has been circumscribed as a large gamut of blueprints for attaining important results all the while averting inappropriate behaviors in the entire school population (Sugai, Horner, & Todd, 2000).

The PBS program is a prevention program designed to prevent violence and other student code of conduct infractions that may result in suspensions. The main intent of the PBS program is to teach students that there are consequences to every decision. Students learn that, although poor decisions reap negative consequences, good choices reap rewards. Students are taught more appropriate ways to deal with undesirable situations, and they are made aware that everything they do is a choice and every action has a positive or negative consequence. Thus, when they choose to do something, they choose to accept the consequences that come with that action.

Definition of Terms

The following specific terms that were used in the study are defined.

Aberrant behavior checklist (ABCL) measures the intensity of the target behaviors (Feeney & Ylvisaker, 2008).

Antecedent strategy is a behavior approach with advantages such as prevention of problematic behavior from occurring through the modification of the environmental events that forego inappropriate behavior, tendency to be quick acting, the capability to fix an atmosphere that is contributing to inappropriate behavior, and the improvement of the learning environment.

Behavior modification is based on the idea that maladaptive patterns depend on learning processes and, as such, can be unlearned (Eli, Baht, & Blacher, 2004).

Check-in and checkout approach is when a student communicates with a assigned adult in the morning to create goals that govern how the student will behave throughout the day. The student will be provided with a point card that will give opportunities for other adults to give feedback on the student's behavior throughout the day. At the end of the day, the student will, then, go back to his or her assigned adult and review the feedback that was given. Finally, the point card is given to the parents to review and sign at home and return to school (Filter et al., 2007).

Classroom is characterized by a type of adult-child relationship (close or conflicting) where there is a continuum from positive, prosocial environments to angry, hostile environments (Howes, 2000).

Coaches' checklist is a checklist that gives continuous information about the coaches' ability to assist school teams administer the important parts of the PBS program (Barrett, Bradshaw, & Lewis-Palmer, 2008).

Context, input, process, and product (CIPP) is a comprehensive framework used in evaluation of programs (Stufflebeam, 1971).

Discrete trial training involves taking a specific skill and breaking it down into parts and continually trying to master each part until the skill is mastered.

Effective behavior support can be used to figure out how much implementation is needed and how important change is in all areas of the PBS program (Horner et al., 2004).

Implementation Phases Inventory is a means to certify each phase of PBS implementation and keep data of the progress the school is making toward maintaining and sustaining a school-wide program.

Intervention Effectiveness Evaluation scale measures the effectiveness of PBS interventions (Feeney & Ylvisaker, 2008).

Office discipline referral (ODR) is a method used by schools to track and control inappropriate behavior. It is an atypical metric that depicts a specific situation where a child engages in inappropriate behavior that violates what is expected of him/her is caught and the administrative staff delivers a repercussion through a document that defines what happened (Sprague, Sugai, Horner, & Walker, 1999).

PBS is the identification of inappropriate behavior within which teacher come together to find more effective interventions (Hendley, 2007).

Pivotal response training encourages child motivation by giving the child choices, reinforcing attempts, and reviewing previously mastered tasks.

Suspension rates are suspension data that help explore the association between training in the PBS program and student discipline problems by comparing preintervention and postintervention suspension data for the elementary and middle schools that were trained in using the school-wide PBS program (Barrett et al., 2008).

Team Implementation Checklist (TIC) is a 26-item checklist that can be used to assess information about activities related to the critical features of the PBS program and to monitor the school's progress in the PBS action plan implementation (Barrett et al., 2008).

Summary

It was clear from the suspension reports that students at School A exhibited a need for some type of behavioral prevention program. Now that the program was in place, it was important to determine the effectiveness of the PBS program.

CHAPTER 2

Literature Review

In the United States, teachers encounter problems with the students' behavior. The problems often arise in the classroom between teachers and students because of the existence of a socioemotional climate. According to Howes (2000), the socioemotional climate has levels of aggression and behavioral problems that affect the nature of student- teacher relationship, and the frequency and complexity of play with peers. A classroom is a type of adult-student relationship (close or conflicting) with a continuum from positive, prosocial environments, to angry, hostile environments (Howes, 2000). Close relationships commonly lead to the former, whereas conflicting relationships usually lead to the latter. Thus, the teacher has the crucial responsibility of shaping the socioemotional climate in the classroom (Rydell & Henricsson, 2004). Several researchers suggested that a teacher with a warm personality could help prevent student's decisions to quit school, unacceptable actions, and he/she could help promote student academic success (Hamilton & Howes, 1992; Pianta, Steinberg, & Rollins, 1995).

In the teaching profession, human resource personnel look for people who are knowledgeable of current trends in classroom management (Wheldall & Beaman, 1998). However, unfortunately this knowledge is not common among education professionals. A large amount of teachers have confessed to not having the skills and knowledge necessary to handle inappropriate behaviors and therefore many students with disabilities are not included in the classroom environment effectively. Often times, these inappropriate behaviors are the reason cited for teachers leaving the classroom. Relieving stress is a big part of keeping teachers in the classroom, but even this is not enough. Ultimately, the solution to the problem is the address the issue causing the stress, inappropriate behavior.

Research has proven that teachers are disturbed by the idea of dealing with aggressive and disruptive behavior (Eli et al., 2004). Ironically, part of the job description of being a teacher in today's society includes dealing with inappropriate behaviors (Hagekull & Hammarberg, 2004). As a matter of fact, some children will forever exhibit uncontrolled behaviors if teachers are unsuccessful with dealing with them when they are young (Rydell & Henricsson, 2004).

A successful, positive behavior program may depend on the awareness of teachers of the difficulties that students with developmental disabilities constantly experience. According to Clements and Martin (2002), people with developmental disabilities are often suffering from the state of powerlessness. They have problems communicating verbally and, often, fail to defend themselves from verbal attacks of normal people. The reason is because developmental problems impact their capacity to process verbal input; the capacity to produce verbal output; and the capacity to formulate verbally thoughts, feelings, and interpretations. They have difficulties challenging opinions about them, explaining the situation, or putting a point of view in a way that is likely to influence what is being said about them. Thus, it is very easy for the judgments of others to determine what happens in that individual's life (Clements & Martin, 2002). They are discriminated as stupid, irrational, childlike, and incapable of thinking and solving problems.

Another cause of their powerlessness is their economic conditions. Clements and Martin (2002) stated that most people or children with developmental disabilities come from poor families. As children of poor parents, they will find it hard to choose who provides services to them, who supports them on a day-to-day basis, who provides health care, and with which psychologist or psychiatrist they feel comfortable working (Clements & Martin, 2002). People with developmental disorders also suffer lives of constant scrutiny. They are often watched and observed, and, often, people do not trust their abilities (Clements & Martin, 2002). Unfortunately, people often see the bad in them instead of the good, and this always results in discrimination and scrutiny that can greatly affect the quality of their daily lives (Clements & Martin, 2002). People with developmental disabilities are much more likely than others to be identified as having problematic behavior. For that identification to become public and for it to be followed by professional efforts will intrude into people's lives whether they like it or not.

Because it is easy to scrutinize children for having serious behavior and developmental disorders due to actions they specifically commit, Clements and Martin (2002) listed some points on how to justify identifying someone with developmental problems. Clements and Martin stated that a behavior is significantly unacceptable if it meets at least one of the following criteria:

1. It is illegal, and the law concerned is usually enforced.
2. If anyone else did this, there would be sustained efforts by those involved with the person to effect change.
3. The behavior is likely to inflict demonstrable costs on the life of the person.
4. The behavior is likely to inflict demonstrable costs on the lives of others who have a right to be free from such imposed costs.
5. The behavior should be continuing despite informal efforts to draw the problem to the person's attention and to effect some change. (p. 19)

Basically, it is not proper to consider a student as someone with a developmental disorder just because his or her behavior is irritable to classmates or teachers. There should be proper criteria on considering an individual with a developmental disorder.

Problem Behaviors

Teachers constantly encounter various problem behaviors from their students.

Members of the SAMHA (2003) listed some behavioral disorders that children and adolescents often experience. Behavioral disorders such as anxiety, severe depression, bipolar, ADHD, learning, conduct, eating, autism, and schizophrenia may adversely affect a child's health. Several of the teacher's may possess one or more of the behavior problems. Each behavior problem has different signs and symptoms (Tynan, 2003). On the other hand, students with bipolar disorder may demonstrate exaggerated mood swings that range from extreme highs (e.g., excitedness or manic phases) to extreme lows (e.g., depression; American Psychiatric Association, 1994).

It is more than likely that teachers will experience one or more of the symptoms mentioned above from their students. Overall, they are faced with the great task of identifying and understanding behavior problem symptoms and applying effective disciplinary strategies and approaches.

Disciplinary decisions are crucial and difficult. Lack of understanding or knowledge on the behavioral problems of students may lead to disproportionate exclusion (Achilles, McLaughlin, & Croninger, 2007). Researchers who conducted several studies reported that students who suffer from emotional and behavioral disorders and learning disabilities received harsher punishments that doubled or even tripled the school population (Achilles et al., 2007; Zhang, Katsiyannis, & Herbst, 2004). Through the use of the Special Education Elementary Longitudinal Study dataset and logistic regression analysis, Achilles et al. (2007) found that students in the primary disability categories of emotional and behavioral disorders and ADHD were more likely than students in the learning disabilities category to have been excluded from school. However, the researchers did not explore the link of teacher disciplinary strategies on the exclusion of those students with serious behavioral problems.

Interventions

One way that school personnel and school district officials address problem behaviors of students effectively is by using a three-tiered approach. The approach calls for the school to identify risk factors (factors that put a person at risk for the disease) and eliminate these factors. It also calls for the school to increase protective factors. School personnel who use the three-tiered approach recommend that students learn proper behaviors, and get an opportunity to use the skills. In addition, all students should receive opportunities to practice the newly learned skills and receive feedback. In most cases, that caring adult is the classroom teacher (Eli et al., 2004).

Another approach is behavior modification. This method is predicated on the idea of changing inappropriate patterns of behavior in a patient. Its justified by the idea that inappropriate behavior patterns have been learned and this information can therefore be unlearned (Eli et al., 2004). Some examples of behavioral modification techniques that can be utilized in an effective program are discrete trial training (DTT; Lovaas, 1987) and pivotal response training (Koegel, Koegel, & Schreibman, 1991). DTT includes pulling a skill apart into several small parts and practicing these components until the skill is mastered, whereas the pivotal response training is almost similar except that it is child centered and driven. This type of training gives children choices, builds off of what they already know, and reinforces attempts.

A good inclusion program may also promote PBS to students with behavioral problems. For instance, classroom practices in inclusive education may include approaches such as cooperative learning, peer tutoring, curriculum-based measurement, collaborative problem solving, and other mixed designs. In cooperative learning, Students with special needs are left in the classroom and are provided with instruction from special education staff. This increases the amount of time allotted to learning, reduces the number of inappropriate behaviors, and gives the students and opportunity to become more active participants in their classrooms. It also provides teachers an opportunity to collaborate and get ideas from one another. On the other hand, students have an opportunity to be paired with students of differing ability groups through peer tutoring. It has proven to help decrease the achievement gap between students with and without disabilities (Fuchs, Fuchs, Mathes, & Simmons, 1997; Kamps, Barbetta, Leonard, & Delquadri, 1994; Stevens & Slavin, 1995a, 1995b).

Kern and Clemens (2007) suggested some strategies to put in place to help prevent inappropriate classroom behavior before it ever occurs. Antecedent strategies have four distinct advantages: prevention of problematic behavior from occurring through modification of the events or environmental stimuli that may have caused the problem behavior, tendency to be quick acting, and enhancement of the instructional environment. Some class wide antecedent strategies include establishing a clear and concise set of rules for the students to follow, increasing the ability to foretell what may happen in the environment, increasing reinforcement of good choices, and presenting material that ensures that all students are receiving a fair and appropriate education (Kern & Clemens, 2007).

The check-in and checkout approach is a recommended behavior intervention program to implement at school (Filter et al., 2007). In the check-in and checkout program, the student meets and review goals daily with an adult. Other teachers provide feedback on the student's behavior. At the end of the day the feedback is reviewed by both the student and assigned adult. The student then takes the card home to be signed by his parents (Filter et al., 2007). Several studies confirmed that the check-in and checkout approach was an effective preventive model of behavioral support (Fairbanks, Sugai, Guardino, & Lathrop; Todd et al., 2008). This program was very attractive because it has an easy implementation process and is effective in decreasing the incidences of inappropriate behavior. In the study by Filter et al. (2007), personnel and schoolteachers also perceived the check-in and checkout approach as effective.

School-Wide PBS

PBS refers to the importance of identifying maladaptive behaviors within which teachers collaborate to develop more effective, proactive interventions (Hendley, 2007). Some of the aims of PBS are to ensure that all students are learning in a comfortable and safe environment, keeping record of inappropriate behaviors, understanding what is causing the behaviors, helping students in understanding the problems with their behaviors, using visual supports, and allowing students to take responsibility for their actions (Hendley, 2007).

Benedict, Horner, and Squires (2007) examined PBS in the schools. One of their objectives was to assess how teachers felt about participating in PBS study. The results showed that teachers believed that PBS consultation was excellent and could be recommended to other teachers in the field. On the contrary, no significance was found between PBS implementation and improvement in students' behavior. The lack of time in the study was pointed out as one of the reasons why such significance was not found.

Mesibov, Browder, and Kirkland (2002) explored the use of individualized schedules as a component of PBS. Teaching students to use schedule boards in performing tasks may help in eliminating disruptive behavior during transition (Mesibov et al., 2002). Previous findings showed that problem behaviors increased when schedules became unpredictable (Flannery & Horner, 1994). Although potentially capable of improving PBS, Mesibov et al. suggested that more research was needed to prove its significance with problem behavior improvement. Further, students should be trained to use an individualized schedule pattern. Mesibov et al. recommended the use "of the Treatment and Education of Autistic and Related Communication Handicapped Children (TEACCH) approach to reduce the training time of students" (p. 76). TEACCH is a statewide parent-professional collaborative program that serves individuals with autism (Mesibov et al., 2002). The TEACCH program combines behavioral techniques and cognitive social learning strategies (e.g., environmental modifications) within a developmental framework to address autism-specific needs (Mesibov et al., 2002).

Zuna and McDougall (2004) explored the effectiveness of PBS in the management of task avoidance among students. Through a case study approach, the researchers found significance between the two variables. The use of positive verbal reinforcement helped decrease slightly escape-motivated behaviors and attention-seeking behaviors. However, the researchers did not pursue certain research-based standards of practice to get PBS into practice within the classroom. Nonetheless, the case study provided some insight on the effectiveness of PBS to a single student.

McIntosh, Horner, Chard, Boland, and Good (2006) explored the relationship between inappropriate behaviors and reading skills. They also looked into the importance of using assessments to predict which students would not respond to behavior intervention programs in the fifth grade. Through the use of the Office Discipline Referral (ODR) index, the researchers found students who were having academic difficulties were at a greater risk for exhibiting future inappropriate behavior.

Killu, Weber, Derby, and Baretto (2006) explored the adherence to PBS by states in the United States. First, the authors introduced the Individual

With Disabilities and Education Act and its preceding requirements for schools to develop individual interventions plans to treat students with disabilities and behavior problems. Through descriptive research, the researchers found that states are more concerned with manipulation of consequent and antecedent strategies, and establishing a time line for follow-up (Killu et al., 2006).

Lassen, Steele, and Sailor (2006) investigated the link between school-wide PBS and academic achievements in urban middle schools. The researchers confirmed previous results that school-wide PBS implementation reduced suspension. Over a 3-year period, there was a notable increase in standardized test scores in mathematics.

Killu et al. (2006) took a look at the resources that were obtained or created and circulated by state education agencies in all states and analyzed the information by comparing it with standard practice for BIP and PBS program development. The design of the study was descriptive, analyzing all resources and materials that were presented by each state about the implementation and design of BIPs and PBS programs. The study found that most states (73%) agreed that an FBA should be completed prior to a BIP and PBS program and the plan should talk about teaching alternative skills or changing a problem behavior. Further, most states (65%) gave ideas for creating an intervention program based on a idea derived from the results of an FBA, took a look at the need to define the ideal behaviors, and considered which programs would be best to promote the desired outcome.

The most widely addressed issues with the states providing resources included the manipulation of consequent strategies, the manipulation of antecedent strategies, and requirements for ongoing data collection (Killu et al., 2006). In terms of maintenance, the most addressed issues were follow-up of the behavior or establishing a time line for follow-up (Killu et al., 2006).

Cihak, Alberto, and Frederick (2007) studied how schools located and chose which interventions they would use for inappropriate behaviors. Four high school students with disabilities ranging from moderate to severe participated in a study about maintaining contingencies of selected behaviors. After that, the teachers who supervised them were interviewed, and interview results were conducted using brief functional analysis and confirmatory analysis. Cihak et al. found that

> the antecedent-based intervention of self-operated auditory prompts worked as effectively as or better than the response-based intervention. In addition, teachers' social validity of intervention in public settings assessed the acceptability of both interventions. Teachers indicated that auditory prompts were socially acceptable for vocational training in public community settings. (p. 80)

Self-operated auditory prompts (SOAP) was the antecedent- based intervention used for this study. SOAP alters the antecedent conditions by shifting stimulus control from the discriminative-producing event to an alternative stimulus to occasion appropriate social behavior. Based on Cihak et al.' s (2007) literature review, SOAP can help eliminated problem behaviors, vocalizations, being off task, and typical inappropriate behavior. SOAP has been successfully implemented in schools, vocational centers, and public community settings (Cihak et al., 2007).

Scott (2007), on the other hand, explored the problem of individual dignity and social truth in PBS programs that were implemented school wide. Scott defined dignity as where an individual thinks that he/she stands. Predicated on dealings and relationships within the environment, social validity was qualified by the complete network defined in terms of the system as a whole. The author was trying to make it clear that, without thinking of individual dignity and social truth, a PBS program can never be successful. First, Scott argued that PBS is individualized because it is decided by the neutralization between the rational and what is naturalistic and useful for the stakeholders to implement securely. He also argued that PBS is about consensus among stakeholders. However, to promote dignity and social validity, a public forum must be used for making decisions, and these decisions must be based on each individual situation. There is also a consensus that those who make these decisions are responsible for the results of their decisions. It is also important for school personnel to listen to stakeholders' voices to make sure that all systemic decisions fit contextually and are relevant.

In evidence-based practice, prevention efforts should create success without embarrassing or creating constraint or pain if the teachers are careful to make sure that they take into consideration the dignity of all participants in the PBS (Scott, 2007). Another important element that Scott (2007) mentioned was effective instruction. He argued that effective instruction could be a bridge to promoting dignity in prevention intervention programs. That is because instruction that works not only makes the student successful but it also creates a sense of independence. Measuring success and change is also important. Scott explained that making the public aware that the practice is creating the outcome can guarantee that the public stand behind the program, whereas individual dignity can be protected by using data to make decisions.

One of the widely used PBS models was the Maryland statewide PBS model. It means of achieving school-wide discipline that was created better allow staff to employ practices that have been validated by research. Following the same methods used in public health, it uses a wide range of service for youths who seemingly do not respond normal discipline by offering practice in programs that have evidence to support their success for at risk students. It also facilitates collaboration outside agencies including mental health specialists (Barrett et al., 2008).

The Maryland statewide PBS model comes with statewide evaluation efforts to determine the progress of each implementation. One of the issues with the evaluation effort is the fidelity of implementation. This variable is measured by using the TIC, the Coaches' Checklist, and the SET (Barrett et al., 2008). The SET revealed high levels of fidelity across Maryland schools. This leads educators to believe that Maryland schools are seeing a lower rate of ODRs in all grade levels. Further, there were considerable decreases in suspension rates. This suggests one who uses a PBS should expect lower suspension rate after little as one year of implementation (Barrett et al., 2008).

The TIC is a 26-item checklist that can be instrumental in finding out information about PBS activities and to monitor the school's progress in PBS action plan implementation (Barrett et al., 2008). This self-assessment tool--to be answered by team leaders--rates items as completed, still working on it, or not yet begun (Barrett et al., 2008).

On the other hand, the Coaches' Checklist is a checklist that gives takes a look at a Coach's capability to assist staff in putting the important parts of the PBS program into play. This checklist is scored with "Yes" or "No" across 13 items to show the prescence lack of presence of each portion (Barrett et al., 2008).

Finally, the SET is based solely on a couple hours of constant observation a PBS program. This observation is conducted by an independent observer (Barrett et al., 2008). Its purpose and advantages were discussed previously.

For outcome measures, Barrett et al. (2008) specified the use of ODRs and suspension rates. ODR data can be acquired through the Internet-based, school-wide information system that, basically, helps school personnel keep track of data on inappropriate behaviors and come up with reports and charts that are utilized to make program decisions. On the other hand, suspension rates refer to suspension data that help investigate the relationship between training in PBS and school wide behavior problems by comparing suspension data from before the program was implemented and after the program's implementation for school personnel who were trained in school-wide PBS (Barrett et al., 2008).

Training and needs assessment were also conducted using a simple descriptive research. It included three groups of headings (school-wide PBS, secondary programs, and external collaborations) and 18 training areas (Barrett et al., 2008).

Mass-Galloway, Panyan, Smith, and Wessendorf (2008) wrote an article that shared the results of their school-wide PBS in Iowa and also offered a model to show how the results of their study guide their work. Iowa's PBS model, a 5-year evaluation plan, was a collective effort between Drake University, Iowa State University, the Research Institute for Studies in Education, the Iowa Federation of Families for Children's Mental Health, and the Iowa Department of Education. Some of the important variables that the plan aimed to monitor were the capability of the school personnel to adapt the model with fidelity, the capability of the model to affect problem behavior patterns, and how the program affects the possibility of personnel to put more behavior modification programs in place (Mass-Galloway et al., 2008).

Mass-Galloway et al. (2008) used the SET and the TIC for addressing whether the school personnel could adopt school-wide PBS with dedication.

The SET was given by an outside observer, and the TIC was completed by the school personnel (Mass-Galloway et al., 2008). The assessments were conducted on four cohorts. Cohort 1 included eight demonstration sites in the fall of 2002, Cohort 2 added 24 more sites in 2004, Cohort 3 included 24 more sites in 2005, and Cohort 4 added 29 more sites in 2006. The results revealed problem behavior patterns. Group 2 had seen more ODRs during that study years, while the other groups had a decrease in ODRs. Although the Iowa school- wide PBS is still in its initial process, the results showed that the program is becoming successful. There is more and more evidence that school-wide PBS programs that are implanted create positive outcomes (Mass-Galloway et al., 2008).

Franzen and Kamps (2008) took a look at how the implementation of an intervention that used recess affected inappropriate behavior on a playground at an urban elementary school. The method used in the research was descriptive research. The dependent variables were behaviors of students and teachers. The the student behaviors that were focused on were general disruption, not using playground equipment properly, fighting, and foul language. For teachers, the study focused on behaviors that included supervision and discipline. Data collection was completed based off of the number of instances each inappropriate behavior was displayed in a 5-minute period of time that the observation took place (Franzen & Kamps, 2008).

The results of the study were positive. Some physical behaviors such as physical horse playing was significantly reduced for students in the second and fourth grade, and students in the third grade saw a slight drop in this inappropriate play too. There was also significant drops in the amount of fighting that took place in all grades. The program as a whole contributed to less negative teacher-student interactions, and teachers were becoming more effective at watching what was happening on the school playgrounds. It was also found that students were more cooperative in their interactions with each other (Franzen & Kamps, 2008).

Muscott, Mann, and LeBrun (2008) explored the effects of the implementation of a PBS program on students' discipline and academic achievement in a school in New Hampshire. The instruments that were used to study the validity of the program were the Universal Team Checklist, the Effective Behavior Support Survey, and the SET. The SET revealed that 15 of 28 programs (54%) were at least 80% effective in lowering the number of ODRs within 3 months of their implementation. The overall results showed that the programs that were in place in New Hampshire were adapting well to the practices of the school-wide PBS program and not only did it effectively reduce the number of ODRs in the 1st year, but it also was able to sustain this pattern for the next (Muscott et al., 2008).

The comparison of ODRs also showed significant results. The results revealed that the New Hampshire PBS project was successful in creating a school-wide discipline system that supported the positive behavior of the majority of the student population and continued to be a vital program for several years (Muscott et al., 2008). Mathematics achievements also significantly increased based on the SET results. An overwhelming majority of elementary, multilevel, and high schools where the school-wide PBS with fidelity was implemented also demonstrated a high level of achievement mathematics (Muscott et al., 2008). However, reading achievement improvement was only average. Muscott et al. (2008) noted that improvements in reading and language scores were found in only nine of 22 schools (41%) that achieved 80% on the SET.

Barriers and Facilitation

Kincaid, Childs, Blasé, and Wallace (2007) conducted a case study on the barriers in implementing the school-wide PBS. The subject was Florida's PBS project that, according to Kincaid et al., was designed to get a better understanding of obstacles and issues that prevented schools from successfully implementing PBS programs.

Kincaid et al. (2007) evaluated and revised training curricula annually as they studied how loyal school staff was to the implementation of the PBS program. They used the SET as their instrument in this study. Personnel at each participating and implementing school were also given the benchmarks of quality and required to complete it. The purpose of the BOQ is to measure how faithfully school personnel are implementing the school-wide PBS (Kincaid et al., 2007).

The results of the study revealed that highly important barriers included staff "buy-in," data, staff implementation, reward systems, implementation issues, and time (Kincaid et al., 2007). These were found to be highly important for high implementers and low implementers of the PBS (Kincaid et al., 2007). On the other hand, the highly feasible and highly important barriers that high implementers and low implementers found were buy-in and misperceptions about school-wide PBS and data issues.

Highly important strengths of project roles were identified as school district officials' support, Florida PBS project support, facilitators, support from guardians and parents and community. On the other hand, highly important strength of the Florida PBS project to impact included school district officials' support, Florida PBS project support, use of data, and administrative support (Kincaid et al., 2007).

Research Questions

The intent of this study was to measure the improvement, if any, in student behavior as a result of their participation in the PBS program. The primary research question was, what is the impact of the PBS program on student's behavior?

The subsequent research questions were

1. What is the overall opinion of this program amongst the stakeholders?
2. What is the role of each stakeholder group (parents, teachers, students, administration, and community) in implementing this program?
3. What changes must be made, if any, to make the PBS program more effective in curbing the number of suspensions in School A?
4. Has the number of student infractions decreased as a result of the PBS program?
5. Has the number of repeat offenders decreased as a result of the PBS program?

Summary

The assertions in some of the literature review were supportive of the previous findings that the PBS program is related to decreases in behavioral problems in schools. There are other programs such as the Second Step, Stop and Think Social Skills Intervention, and Parents-Teachers Action Research. Each of these approaches has its own strengths and weaknesses.

Chapter 3

Methodology

The researcher's focus was to investigate the effect that the PBS program had on student code of conduct violations. An outcomes-based program evaluation was utilized. In a simple logic model, inputs, outputs, and outcomes were identified. To determine these components, suspension data from the 2003-2004 to the 2007-2008 school years were utilized. The researcher surveyed teachers (see Appendix A), parents (see Appendix B), and students (see Appendix C) involved in this program to gather their perceptions of the program's effectiveness. Other data were extracted from the referrals made by teachers, administrators, and other appropriate school personnel. The instruments that were used in the survey were self-designed questionnaires with elements based on several instruments mentioned in the literature review such as the Effective Behavior Support Survey, Student Climate Survey, ODRs, TIC, Implementation Phases Inventory, and the Behavior Support Survey. The results from the questionnaires are presented via tables, charts, and graphs. Data from the Delaware Department of Education school profiles and individuals' school records were used to assist in the triangulation of data. In addition, archival data regarding the school's code of conduct violations was available to the researcher for comparative purposes.

Sampling Size

The sampling size of the research was determined using Creswell's (2002) sample error formula. It is an approach used in surveys when seeking to generalize results from a sample to a population. It is based on stating the amount of sampling error the researcher is willing to tolerate.

In this study, 5% of sampling error was tolerated from a population of 74 participants. Thus, to meet the sampling error, 71 participants were required to provide complete answers for every question in the questionnaire.

Sampling Methods

In this study, nonprobability sampling was used to give the researcher more freedom to choose the respondents who were most suitable to participate in the study. Basically, it provided a range of alternative techniques based on the researcher's subjective judgment.

Specifically, the nonprobability sampling that was used in the study was snowball sampling (Saunders, Lewis, & Thornhill, 2003). Snowball sampling refers to a technique used when it is difficult to identify members of the desired population. In this study, it was difficult to determine which teachers actively participated properly in a PBS program in this school. Therefore, the following steps were used to select the samples: made contact with one or two cases in the population, asked them to identify further cases, asked the new cases to identify further cases, and repeated the steps until no new cases were given or the sample was as large as was manageable (Saunders et al., 2003).

Participants

All students, teachers, parents, and administrators who were actively involved in the implementation of this program were a part of the target group. All 376 students in the study school were required to participate in the PBS program; therefore, they all had an opportunity to be involved in the study. The basic demographic information of the participants was that they all came from one urban school setting in the low- to middle-class income communities. Assuming the general demographics of the school district, participants were African American, Asian, Pacific Islanders, Caucasian, and Hispanic and Latino (60% minorities and 40% Caucasian).

A letter of consent was sent to the study school's school district officials to ask for permission to conduct the research. The respondents were 35 teachers who had been teaching in the school for 2 years or more and had experienced the PBS that the school personnel had implemented. Additionally, there were also 14 students and 25 parents who participated in this study.

Variables

The independent variable of the study was the PBS program at the target school. The dependent variables of the study were elements under the CIPP framework.

In the context framework, the dependent variables were the context of the program, the needs and goals of the school to justify the PBS, the objectives of the program, and the proficiency and responsiveness of the objectives to the identified needs. In the input framework, the dependent variables were the program inputs and resources, program performance, design of the program, alternative strategies, and procedures that have been considered for the program.

In the process framework, the following were the dependent variables: implementation of the program, performance of the program, consistency of the program in following guidelines in the ethical and legal domains, and the defects in the procedural design or in the implementation of the program. Finally, in the product framework, the following dependent variables were measured: the general and specific outcomes of the program, the anticipated outcomes, the merit of the program, and the actual worth or value of the program.

Rationale and Justification of the Method

The CIPP model of evaluation (Stufflebeam et al., 2003) provided thorough information about the nature of PBS within the school that was selected for survey. Based on the CIPP framework and several cited PBS instrument measures, the surveys were able to produce results that answered the research questions of the study and more. The surveys had the potential to answer the overall opinions of the stakeholders about the program, the role of each stakeholder groups, the effectiveness of the program, and other results that fell within the CIPP of the program. The study was cross-sectional because of the limited time and resources available to conduct the surveys. Self-design surveys using variables from different PBS instruments were appropriate. The SET, for instance, was pervasive and required more time and respondents to conduct; thus, it was inappropriate to use for the study.

Instrumentation

The variables in this research were explored using a quantitative approach to evaluate the data gathered. The independent variable of the study was the PBS, whereas the dependent variable was the effectiveness of the PBS implementation, specifically, its impact on suspension rate and ODRs.

Quantitative data refer to numerical or contained data that can be quantified. This type of data can range from simple data to more complex data. Analysis of data from this type can be done in many ways. The researcher can create simple tables that show how often an occurrence happens, or he or she can show more complex statistical modeling (Saunders et al., 2003).

Quantitative analysis cannot exist without statistics because the former needs the latter to verify the data. For example, the researcher has to determine a mode to determine which value occurs more frequently. In other words, during all stages of scientific inquiry, statistics are used (Biemer & Lieberg, 2003).

Context

To evaluate the context of the PBS, a descriptive research involving a series of surveys was conducted. A descriptive study is defined as a design that concerns a univariate question or hypothesis in which researchers ask about and state something about (e.g., the size, form, distribution, or existence of a variable; Cooper & Schindler, 2003). The purpose of this type of study is to project an accurate profile of persons, events, and situations (Saunders et al., 2003). It is useful to describe the phenomena associated with the subject population, estimate the proportion of the population that shares the same characteristics, and discover the association between dependent and independent variables (Cooper & Schindler, 2003).

The first measure that was used was a closed-ended survey that addressed the following: (a) context of the program, (b) the needs and goals of the school to justify the PBS, (c) the objectives of the program, and (d) the proficiency and responsiveness of the objectives to the identified needs. Firsthand data were acquired from each school respondent. Materials and manuals used in the program were requested to determine the overall context of the program and its stated objectives. The results were presented in table format in the actual study.

Second, the four statements mentioned above were addressed by surveying teachers from the study school in Delaware where the PBS had been implemented. The survey was in a rating or scale question format. This format is often used to collect opinion data. Further, the opinions of all of the participants of the research were needed in the study to determine the proficiency of the objectives to be responsive enough to the needs of the school. The rating surveys had a 5-point Likert scale of *agree, tend to agree, uncertain, tend to disagree,* and *disagree* (Saunders et al., 2003). Basically, by using the Likert scale, the researcher asked the respondent how strongly they agreed or disagreed with a statement or series of statements. The results were analyzed through descriptive analysis wherein the weighted mean was used to determine the level of agreement or disagreement of the general samples (Saunders et al., 2003).

Input

Similar to the context variables, the input variables were measured using descriptive research. The following elements were evaluated in this part: (a) program inputs and resources, (b) comparison of program performance,

(c) evaluation of the design of the program, and (d) examination of what alternative strategies and procedures for the program should be considered.

A self-assessment, semistructured questionnaire is a list of questions that is used to gather information on a specific research topic. The reason a questionnaire is used is so that the researcher can ask all of the participants the same questions and compare their answers. These self-assessment, semistructured surveys were constructed and distributed to the parents of students and the teachers to determine program inputs and resources. The program manual or document was also reviewed to determine the intention of the program.

The following were specific dependent variables explored in this part: (a) the literature or previous programs on which the program was based, (b) the model used in designing the program, (c) the people who participated in the program, and (d) the number of students who had been covered by the program. The surveys were analyzed through descriptive analysis, and results for the study school were compared using a one-way ANOVA test.

Process

The process stage was used to explore the following variables: (a) how the program was implemented, (b) how the program was performing, and (c) the defects in the procedural design or in the implementation of the program. These processes were explored using surveys.

The research survey was completed by chosen school staff on their own time, students, and parents at home. Completion of survey was voluntary. Staff, parents, and students had the right to decline if they did not want to participate in the survey. Administration of the surveys took place at the beginning of the school year after receipt of Institutional Review Board (IRB) approval. The survey was completed independently (Sugai et al., 2000). The respondents should have based their ratings on their individual experiences in school or answered the questions that were only applicable to them (Sugai et al., 2000). In the study, several elements of the effective behavior support were used in the survey, and the researcher employed a 5-point Likert scale to survey the process of the program.

Product

The product phase was used to assess the outcome of the project and if it was worth continuing or should have been reformatted. In this stage, the following variables were assessed: (a) the general and specific outcomes of the program, (b) the anticipated outcomes, (c) the merit of the program< and (d) the actual worth or value of the program.

Data Analysis

Data were analyzed by a data analyst using the latest Statistical Package for Social Sciences software. Descriptive results were presented in table format.

Time Line

Upon IRB approval, the researcher began this study. Data were gathered from referral records; survey of parents, students, and teachers were conducted; and suspension data were gathered. This was completed after IRB approval starting in mid-September 2009, and all the data collection continued through November 2009; all of the data were analyzed.

CHAPTER 4

Results

Each research question was answered by analyzing the responses provided by the participants in the survey, which included faculty members, parents, and students. The distribution of the responses for each statement and for each respondent group was provided, along with the textual explanation of the answers to the research questions. These quantitative data were supplemented by including responses gathered from the participants in the study through open-ended survey questions.

Research Question 1

Research Question 1 asked, What is the overall opinion of this program among the stakeholders? This research question was answered using the responses from participating faculty, parents, and students to Statements 2, 3, and 4 on each of the appropriate surveys. Out of 35 faculty respondents, 18 faculty respondents (51.4%) tended to agree with Statement 2 that stated, "The students, faculty, and parents fully supported this program." Only seven of 35 faculty respondents (20.0%) said that they completely agreed with this statement, whereas seven faculty members (20.0%) expressed uncertainty regarding the statement.

In contrast, 14 out of 25 parent respondents (56.0%) agreed that the parents fully supported the program. Six parent respondents (24.0%) tended to agree with the statement, whereas four parent respondents (16.0%) expressed uncertainty. The largest portion of the student respondents were divided between agreement and uncertainty. Out of 14 student respondents, five students (35.7%) specified their agreement that the student body fully supported the program. Another five students (35.7%) responded with uncertainty regarding Statement 2 of the survey, whereas three student respondents (21.4%) tended to agree with the statement. This information is shown Table 4.

Table 4

Responses to Statement 2: "The Students, Faculty, and Parents Fully Supported This Program."

Category	Faculty		Parents		Students	
	N	*%*	*N*	*%*	*N*	*%*
Agree	7	20.0	14	56.0	5	35.7
Tend to agree	18	51.4	6	24.0	3	21.4
Uncertain	7	20.0	4	16.0	5	35.7
Tend to disagree	3	8.6	0	0.0	0	0.0
Disagree	0	0.0	1	4.0	1	7.1

Although the surveys were used to gather perceptions regarding stakeholder support for the program, the comments made at the bottom of the surveys focused on faculty support for the PBS program. There were no comments made about parent or student support for the program. There were a total of nine comments from faculty about faculty support, seven of which were statements from faculty that expressed the perception that the program was negatively affected by the fact that not all of the faculty members were fully participating in the program.

Three out of six faculty respondents' comments indicated the need for teachers to have a better understanding of the program. These three faculty respondents also believed that there was a need for the faculty members to be more consistent with the Implementation of the program. This idea was best expressed by one of the faculty respondents who stated, "I think, in order to have an effective program, you need everybody on board and everybody doing the same exact thing." Out of nine faculty respondents who made comments, only two expressed that they perceived that the staff fully supported the program. Also in the survey comments, six parent respondents indicated that the faculty and staff were not fully on board with the program. One such parent respondent stated that there were "quite a few teachers who do not give out the paws (certificates students receive for making good choices)." There were no comments made by the students.

Statement 3, "There were enough resources to implement and maintain this program properly," was utilized to determine the perceptions of the faculty, parents, and students about whether there were enough resources to implement the program at home or at school. Twelve out of 35 faculty respondents (34.3%) disagreed with this statement, whereas 11 of them (31.4%) tended to agree with this statement. Six faculty respondents (17.1%) disagreed with the statement, whereas four faculty respondents (11.4%) expressed uncertainty, and only two faculty respondents (5.7%) agreed with the statement.

As for the parent respondents, 10 out of 25 parent respondents (40.0%) agreed that there were enough resources to implement the lessons of the program properly. Eight parent respondents (32.0%) tended to agree with the statement, whereas five of them (20.0%) expressed uncertainty. The 14 students were again divided equally between agreeing and expressing uncertainty about whether there were enough resources to teach the lessons of the program with five student respondents (35.7%) each agreeing and expressing uncertainty. The other four students (28.6%) tended to agree with the statement. This information is shown in Table 5.

Table 5

Responses to Statement 3: "There Were Enough Resources to Implement and Maintain This Program Properly."

	Faculty		Parents		Students	
Category	N	%	N	%	N	%
Agree	2	5.7	10	40.0	5	35.7
Tend to agree	11	31.4	8	32.0	4	28.6
Uncertain	4	11.4	5	20.0	5	35.7
Tend to disagree	12	34.3	1	4.0	0	0.0
Disagree	6	17.1	1	4.0	0	0.0

Ten respondents provided their insight as comments at the end of the survey. Out of these 10, nine faculty respondents expressed the belief that the lack of resources was an obstacle to the effective implementation of the program. One such faculty respondent stated that the available resources for the implementation of the program might not suffice. One faculty respondent stated that the items in the school store, which are used as rewards for students who display proper behavior, "are really important pieces because the students need to see rewards more frequently than once a month." Another faculty respondent suggested tapping the community through fundraisers to help sustain the program financially. One parent also commented in the open-ended portion of the survey that "the program needs more resources." There were no comments from students about this statement. Statement 4, "There were enough staff development opportunities for staff to learn how to teach this program properly," was utilized to gather data on whether the faculty respondents perceived that there were enough opportunities for faculty to learn how to teach the program. The largest portion of faculty respondents or 12 out of 35 faculty respondents (34.3%) expressed disagreement with this statement. In response to Statement 4 on the parents' survey, "There were enough opportunities for parents to learn about this program," 14 out of 25 parents (56.0%) who responded agreed with the statement. Statement 4 of the student survey said, "There were enough opportunities for students to use the skills they learned." Student respondents were once again divided between agreement with the statement and uncertainty about it with six student respondents (42.9%) each agreeing and expressing uncertainty (see Table 6).

Table 6

Responses to Statement 4 for Each Survey

Category	Faculty		Parents		Students	
	N	*%*	*N*	*%*	*N*	*%*
Agree	2	5.7	14	56.0	6	42.9
Tend to agree	10	28.6	2	8.0	2	14.3
Uncertain	6	17.1	6	24.0	6	42.9
Tend to disagree	12	34.3	1	4.0	0	0.0
Disagree	5	14.3	3	8.0	0	0.0

Note. Statement 4 for each survey read, "There were enough staff development opportunities for staff to learn how to teach this program properly," "There were enough opportunities for parents to learn about this program," and "There were enough opportunities for students to use the skills they learned."

The comments made in the faculty surveys focused on whether there were enough staff development opportunities for staff to learn how to teach this program properly. The corresponding statement to this item in the parent surveys dealt with whether there were enough opportunities for the parents to learn how to support this program at home, whereas the corresponding statement in the student survey dealt with whether there were enough resources to support the program. There were no comments in the survey responses submitted by the parents or the student, which means that most of the comments regarding this item were gathered from only the faculty surveys. Seven out of 13 faculty respondents indicated that opportunities were available for them to learn about the program. Three faculty respondents stated that not enough time was provided for the training of teachers for the PBS program, but the responses were not all negative. One faculty respondent expressed optimism because this year "the PBS core team was able to present the program early [and that] there is going to be a big kickoff this school year." Another faculty respondent pointed out that "the actual PBS committee of the district is offering training for our staff." One faculty respondent suggested spacing the training sessions efficiently throughout the year to keep awareness regarding the program on a high level and not to let it get pushed to the back burner because the PBS program "gets lost among the other lessons" that the teachers need to make sure that the students learn such as academics and other behavioral skills. There were no comments from parents or students regarding this statement.

Research Question 2

Research Question 2 asked, What is the role of each stakeholder group (parents, teachers, students, administration, and community) in implementing this program? This research question was answered using the responses of the faculty, parents, and students to Statements 5, 6, and 7 in the survey instruments. The results from Statement 5, "I fully understand all of the goals and objectives of this program," were utilized by the researcher to determine whether the study participants believed that they personally understood the goals of the program. Out of 35 faculty respondents, 14 faculty respondents (40.0%) indicated that they tended to agree with the statement. Out of 25 parent respondents, 11 parent respondents (44.0%) indicated agreement with the statement. The majority of the student respondents or eight out of 14 student participants (57.1%) agreed with the statement. This information is shown in Table 7.

Table 7

Responses to Statement 5: "I Fully Understand All the Goals and Objectives of the Program."

Category	Faculty		Parents		Students	
	N	%	*N*	%	*N*	%
Agree	13	37.1	11	44.0	8	57.1
Tend to agree	14	40.0	6	24.0	2	14.3
Uncertain	6	17.1	6	24.0	4	28.6
Tend to disagree	2	57.4	1	4.0	0	0.0
Disagree	0	0.0	1	4.0	0	0.0

Three responses were gathered from faculty comments on the surveys. These three faculty members who made comments stated that they believed that the faculty members did not completely understand the objectives of the program. One faculty respondent suggested that this might be because the teachers came from different schools and different backgrounds; therefore, they had their own interpretations, and they brought their different ideas to the table. This faculty member said that these diverse ideas were beneficial, but, then, this also meant that not all the teachers were on the same page. There were no comments from students or parents regarding this statement.

The responses of the participants to Statement 6, "I have done my part to help this program become successful," were utilized by the researcher to assess whether the respondents believed that they had done their part to help the program succeed. Based on the data from the surveys, 18 out of 35 faculty respondents (51.4%) agreed with the statement. Similarly, the majority of the student respondents and the parent respondents also expressed agreement. Out of 25 parent respondents, 11 of them

(44.0%) chose *agree*, whereas, out of 14 student respondents, nine student respondents (64.3%) also selected *agree* from the choices (see Table 8).

Table 8

Responses to Statement 6: "I Have Done My Part to Help This Program Become Successful."

Category	Faculty		Parents		Students	
	N	%	N	%	N	%
Agree	18	52.4	11	44.0	9	64.3
Tend to agree	13	37.2	8	32.0	3	21.4
Uncertain	1	2.9	2	8.0	2	14.3
Tend to disagree	3	8.6	1	4.0	0	0.0
Disagree	0	0.0	3	12.0	0	0.0

In the comments, one teacher referred to various tasks that were performed to help implement the program such as giving out paws (certificates that students received when they made good choices) to their students for positive behavior and designing the materials needed for the program apart from making sure that the program was implemented in their own classrooms. Once again, there were no student or parent comments.

The perceptions of the respondents about the administrators' support for the program were assessed through Statement 7 in the survey (see Table 9). For the faculty survey, Statement 7 said, "Administrators are always available to help support staff in any way with this program."

Table 9

Responses to Statement 7: "Administrators Are Always Available to Help Support the Students, Parents, and Staff in Any Way With This Program."

Category	Faculty		Parents		Students	
	N	%	N	%	N	%
Agree	5	14.3	6	24.0	5	35.7
Tend to agree	15	42.9	8	32.0	4	28.6
Uncertain	7	20.0	6	24.0	4	28.6

Tend to disagree	5	14.3	2	8.0	1	7.1
Disagree	3	8.6	3	12.0	0	0.0

Fifteen out of 25 faculty respondents (42.9%) tended to agree with the statement, whereas only five faculty respondents (14.3%) agreed with the statement. The responses from the comments were mixed. Three out of five faculty respondents indicated that the administration members made themselves available for the program, whereas one faculty respondent referred to an incident where a student was taken to the office, but the "administrative doors were closed even though the administration members were inside."

Statement 7 on the parent survey said, "Administrators are always available to help support parents in anyway with this program." The majority of parents, eight out of 25 parents (32%) tended to agree with this statement. Another six parents (24%) completely agreed with this statement. There were no additional comments from the parent participants.

Statement 7 on the student survey said, "Administrators are always available to help support students in any way with this program." Five out of 14 student respondents (35.7%) indicated agreement with this statement. There were no comments made by the students. The information discussed in connection with this research question is shown in Table 9.

Research Question 3

Research Question 3 asked, What changes must be made, if any, to make the PBS program more effective in curbing the number of suspensions in School A? This research question was answered using the responses provided by the study participants to Statement 9, "This program could be more effective if a few changes were made."

Out of 35 faculty respondents, 19 faculty respondents (54.3%) expressed agreement with this statement. Similarly, 11 out of 25 parents (44.0%) expressed agreement with the statement. The student respondents were mostly uncertain about the statement with five out of 14 respondents

(35.7%) selecting *uncertain* from the options. This information is shown in Table 10.

Table 10

Responses to Statement 9: "This Program Could Be More Effective if a Few Changes Were Made."

Category	Faculty		Parents		Students	
	N	*%*	*N*	*%*	*N*	*%*
Agree	19	54.3	11	44.0	5	35.7
Tend to agree	11	31.4	3	12.0	4	28.6
Uncertain	3	8.6	8	32.0	4	28.6
Tend to disagree	2	5.7	2	8.0	1	7.1
Disagree	0	0.0	1	4.0	0	0.0

From the open-ended portion of the surveys, 11 responses were collected from faculty surveys. The responses from the faculty members yielded suggestions about concrete measures through which the PBS program could be improved. Four faculty respondents referred to the importance of having the program really become part of the school community for it to be effective. As one faculty respondent stated in the response, the program should be implemented to the point that "every single person and every single staff member uses the language, uses the incentives, and is consistent throughout the building at all times," which supported the idea that everyone should be on the same page when it came to implementing the program. In connection to this, four faculty respondents cited the importance of having more activities to involve the students in the program and making them more aware and interested in its implementation. As said by a respondent, sometimes the students are not aware of why they are earning the paws. Another faculty respondent also commented that teacher training and involvement should be strengthened.

Research Question 4

Research Question 4 asked, Has the number of student infractions decreased as a result of the PBS program? This research question was answered by using the responses of the participants from Statement 8 on the surveys. Other data were also used to answer Research Question 4, and the data are presented later. In response to Statement 8, 17 of 35 faculty members (48.6%) tended to agree with this statement. Eleven of 25 parents (44.0%) and five of 14 students (35.7%) chose *agree* in response to this statement. This information is presented in Table 11.

Table 11

Responses to Statement 8: "The Program Has Been Effective in Helping Reduce the Number of Student Code of Conduct Infractions."

	Faculty		Parents		Students	
Category	N	%	N	%	N	%
Agree	3	8.6	11	44.0	5	35.7
Tend to agree	17	48.6	6	24.0	4	28.6
Uncertain	8	22.9	7	28.0	4	28.6
Tend to disagree	6	17.1	0	0.0	1	7.1
Disagree	1	2.9	1	4.0	0	0.0

However, the survey measured only the perceptions of the study participants regarding the program's effectiveness. The program's effectiveness was also determined by analyzing the incidence of violations in the student code of conduct (Delaware Department of Education, 2008). The number of behavior referrals went up in all but two types of offenses. Theses two types of offenses were inappropriate sexual behavior and arson for the students in School A during the 2006-2007 and 2007-2008 school years (see Table 12). The information in the table shows that the total number of offenses increased from the 2006-2007 to the 2007-2008 school years, but, by the 2008-2009 school year, a year after the program was implemented, the incidence of behavior referrals decreased further. The number of behavior referrals for the most common offenses such as disruptive behavior increased from 257 referrals in the 2006-2007 school year to 332 in the 2007-2008 school year. For insubordination, the number of referrals increased from 136 to 183 from the 2006-2007 school year to the 2007-2008 school year. For fighting, the number of referrals increased from 83 to 149 from the 2006-2007 school year to the 2007-2008 school year, and the behavior referrals for offensive touching increased from 110 in the 2006-2007 school year to 231 in the 2007-2008 school year.

The data also showed that behavior referrals for these offenses decreased significantly in the 2008-2009 school year, which was the 2nd year of the program's implementation. Behavior referrals for disruptive behavior decreased from 332 in the 2007-2008 school year to just 19 in the 2008-2009 school year. Insubordination also decreased from 183 cases in the 2007-2008 school year to no cases in the 2008-2009 school year. Cases of fighting also decreased from 149 to 96, and cases of offensive touching decreased from 231 to 33 from the 2006-2007 school year to the 2007-2008 school year. It should also be noted that behavior referrals for students using abusive language decreased from 112 cases in the 2006-2007 school year to 75 cases in the 2007-2008 school year to six cases in the 2008-2009 school year.

Table 12

Summary of Behavior Referrals for Various Offenses Across Three School Years

	School year		
Offense	**2006 - 2007**	**2007 – 2008**	**2008 - 2009**
Abusive language to students	112	75	6
Class cutting	0	10	15
Disruptive behavior	257	332	19
Insubordination	136	183	0
Leaving school without permission	0	1	0
Offensive language to staff	0	8	0
Bullying	35	40	0
Fighting	83	149	96
Inappropriate materials	0	1	0
Inappropriate sexual behavior	3	1	0
Instigation	0	3	0
Offensive touching	110	231	33
Sexual harassment	3	11	3
Threatening behavior to staff	0	2	0
Vandalism	0	7	0
Arson	1	1	0
Assault	0	1	0
Offensive touching to staff	10	78	39
Possession of drugs, tobacco, or alcohol	0	3	0
Robbery or extortion	0	1	3
Possession or concealment of weapons	0	7	0

Research Question 5

Research Question 5 asked, Has the number of repeat offenders decreased as a result of the PBS program? The number of repeat offenders was only five in the 2006-2007 school year, the year before the PBS program was implemented in School A (see Table 13). In the 2007-2008 school year, when the PBS program was first launched in October 2007, the number of repeat offenders increased from five to 103. This represented a 1,960.00% increase in the number of offenders. The number of repeat offenders also increased in the succeeding year from 103 in the 2007-2008 school year to 111 in the 2008-2009 school year, which represented a 7.77% increase over the year.

Table 13

Repeat Offenders From the 2004-2005 School Year to the 2008-2009 School Year

School year	No. of repeat offenders
2004-2005	0
2005-2006	41
2006-2007	5
2007-2008	103
2008-2009	111

Summary

The results of the analysis of the data gathered in this study were discussed in chapter 4. Based on the data analysis, the five research questions were answered using the data submitted by the participants. The responses provided by the participants to the Comments section found at the end of each survey instrument were also used to supplement the findings of the quantitative analysis.

CHAPTER 5

Conclusions and Recommendations

The findings and the corresponding implications of the results of the data analysis are discussed by the researcher in this chapter. The researcher also discusses the significance of the study, its limitations, and recommendations for future researchers. The main purpose of this study was to evaluate whether the implementation of the PBS program had an effect on student code of conduct violations in a Delaware school (School A) serving students from Grades 4 through 6. Data were gathered from one survey instrument administered to 74 respondents composed of 35 faculty respondents, 25 parent respondents, and 14 student respondents. Descriptive statistics using the data from the surveys were used to answer Research Questions 1, 2, and 3 that dealt with perceptions of the stakeholders about their overall opinions of the program, their respective roles, particularly of the faculty and administration members, in implementing the program and the changes that needed to be made to the program to make it more effective in curbing suspensions. The major stakeholders who participated in the study included 74 faculty members, parents, and students. Through the surveys, these 74 respondents were able to provide their perceptions on the program, which were supplemented by the responses given in the open-ended part of the survey.

Research Questions 4 and 5 that dealt with the effectiveness of the program in curbing student infractions and repeat offenders were answered using 3 years' worth of data on office referrals, suspensions, and repeat offenders. Responses from the study participants were also used by the researcher to describe the faculty, parent, and student respondents' perceptions regarding the aspects of the program covered by Research Questions 1, 2 and 3. The data covered the 2006-2007 school year, before the program was implemented, until the 2007-2008 school year, the year after the program was first implemented in School A. The researcher expected that the PBS program would have a positive effect on the student code of conduct violations.

Research Question 1

Research Question 1 asked, What is the overall opinion of this program among the stakeholders? The researcher identified three major stakeholders for the PBS program, specifically the faculty members, the parents, and the students. Individuals from these three stakeholder groups participated in the study. Based on the responses of the participants on the surveys and the information provided by the participants who were interviewed, conflicting views on the matter were revealed. The analysis of the results of the survey showed that the parents and students believed that the PBS program was supported by the parents and the student body of School A. On the contrary, when asked about faculty and staff support for the program, some faculty respondents stated that not all faculty members were fully supportive of the program. In the open-ended question portion of the survey, seven respondents stated that they believed that not all teachers were fully participating in the program and that this lackluster support had a detrimental effect on the effectiveness of the program.

Three faculty respondents expressed that they believed that there was a need for a better understanding of the program and how it was supposed to be implemented and a need for consistency. According to one faculty respondent, the school should make sure that the faculty and staff members are all on the same page when it comes to implementing the PBS program. When asked about whether there were enough resources to implement the program, the majority of the faculty members tended to disagree.

In addition, eight faculty respondents specifically stated that the lack of resources was a hindrance to the efficient implementation of the program. In connection to this, although the major stakeholders believed that the program was supported by parents and the student body, there were some faculty members who believed that there were some teachers who did not fully support the program. Based on the comments from the open-ended comment section of the survey, school administrators might need to strengthen efforts to ensure that the faculty members have a uniform understanding of the program, specifically, its goals and the manner by which it should be implemented to increase the success rate of the PBS program. Some faculty respondents believed that there were not enough staff development opportunities to teach them how to implement the program properly. Out of nine faculty members who made comments, three respondents referred to the lack of time to train the faculty and staff properly, and one referred to the need to ensure that the program is not pushed to the back burner of school awareness. There was an expressed hope during the survey from one faculty respondent for an improved training program in the upcoming school year.

The faculty respondents also expressed the perception that there were not enough resources to implement the program properly. The researcher, then, concluded that this was another area of improvement that the school administration should focus on to help implement the PBS program effectively.

The faculty members expressed a different opinion from the parents and the students regarding the PBS program. This led the researcher to conclude that there might be a need to address the concerns raised by the teachers regarding the program because, among the three major stakeholders, it was the faculty members who were able to see the two aspects of the program from its goals and desired manner of implementation to the actual outcome of the program. Therefore, the feedback given by the faculty members regarding the program merits the attention of the school administrators in the hopes of increasing the program's success rate.

Research Question 2

Research Question 2 asked, What is the role of each stakeholder in implementing this program? To address this research question, the researcher assessed whether the faculty members, parents, and students had a proper understanding of the goals and objectives of the program. The comments revealed that three out of 11 faculty respondents expressed that they believed that some teachers did not fully understand the program and its goals. One faculty respondent attributed this to the fact that the teachers came from diverse backgrounds that resulted in a program wherein all the major players such as the faculty members were not on the same page. However, the data showed that each stakeholder group believed that they had done their part to ensure the success of the program. In the survey, one teacher referred to the tasks in the program for which he or she was responsible, which ranged from ensuring the implementation of the program inside the classroom to preparing the materials needed for the program. This is significant because it can be interpreted to mean that there is no clear list of tasks that outline what responsibilities each stakeholder group has to fulfill to help implement the program successfully. Also, out of five open-ended responses gathered, two faculty respondents expressed the perception that the administration did not make itself available to support the program and the students.

The responses from the faculty and administration respondents showed that, although they believed they individually did their parts in implementing the program, they also believed that the other individuals did not necessarily fulfill their roles. Some other faculty respondents referred to the need for the administrators to show support for the program. This led the researcher to conclude that, although each stakeholder believed that they were fulfilling their roles in ensuring the success of the program, more effort and input might be needed from each individual to implement the PBS program properly.

Research Question 3

Research Question 3 asked, What changes must be made, if any, to make the PBS program more effective in curbing the number of suspensions in School A? Among the respondents, faculty and parent respondents believed that some changes could be made to make the program more effective. From the comments, the faculty respondents referred to specific things that the school administrators could do to facilitate the improved implementation of the PBS program.

Out of 11 responses to the open-ended question, 10 implied the need for the better integration of the PBS program into the school community so much so that every single staff member would use the same language and perform the same actions in rewarding good behavior. This observation could be connected to the survey statement regarding staff support and resources for the program. It can also be connected to the suggestion made by one faculty respondent with regard to strengthening teacher training to ensure that all faculty members are consistent in terms of the way they improve the program. Another faculty respondent suggested getting the community involved through fundraisers that may help solve the problem regarding insufficient funding for the program. These measures can be implemented to ensure that the spirit of the PBS program can be internalized by the students by making it a part of the students' way of life. Then, the researcher concluded that school administrators must pay close attention to the integration of the PBS program into the school community to increase its success rates. Based on the recommendations made by the faculty respondents, the researcher also concluded that, aside from the teachers, proper training might also be given to parents to ensure that the PBS program really becomes a part of the students' way of life and not just something that happens in school.

Research Question 4

Research Question 4 asked, Has the number of infractions decreased as a result of the PBS program? The survey responses showed that the faculty respondents, parent respondents, and student respondents believed that the program was effective in terms of reducing violations of behavior referrals. However, this research question is best answered by analyzing the data on behavior referrals. The perceptions of the faculty, parent, and student respondents were somewhat supported by the data on ODRs and suspensions provided for the use of the study.

The data showed that the incidence number of offenses increased from the 2006-2007 school year to the 2007-2008 school year but decreased from the 2007-2008 school year to the 2008-2009 school year. For example, the number of behavior referrals for disruptive behavior increased from 257 in the 2006-2007 school year to 332 in the 2007-2008 school year but decreased to 19 in the 2008-2009 school year. This same pattern was observed in the data for offensive touching and fighting. The offenses increased from the 2006-2007 school year to the 2007-2008 school year and decreased in the 2008-2009 school year. This alone may indicate that the PBS program was effective in decreasing the number of behavior referrals, but another look at the data also showed that there was a consistent increase in suspension cases from the 2006-2007 school year to the 2008-2009 school year (from four to 19 to 134). This led the researcher to conclude that, barring all other factors, the PBS program resulted in a decrease in the number of infractions committed in School A. In connection with this, the researcher also concluded that the conflicting results of the comparison between the data on the violations and the incidence of suspension cases indicated that there was a need for further research to determine whether the program itself was responsible for the decrease in behavior referrals.

Research Question 5

Research Question 5 asked, Has the number of repeat offenders decreased as a result of the PBS program? Despite the mostly positive response expressed by the faculty, parent, and student respondents through the survey regarding their perceptions of the effectiveness of the PBS program and the data on the increase and decrease of the frequencies of student violations from one school year to the next, the data on repeat offenders showed that the implementation of the PBS program did not decrease the number of repeat offenders in School A. The data showed that, since the program's launch in 2007, the number of repeat offenders increased to 103 in comparison to the five repeat offenders in the previous year when the program was not implemented. The increase in repeat offenders continued until the 2008-2009 school year with 113 repeat offenders with the PBS program still in place. This led the researcher to draw the conclusion that the PBS program was ineffective in terms of decreasing the number of repeat offenders per school year.

The data analysis revealed that the perceptions of the respondents regarding the program were positive. Based on the results of the survey, many believed that, although some changes needed to be made to improve its effectiveness, the program was implemented well, was supported by the major stakeholders, and seemed to be an effective behavior intervention program.

The data on the incidence of code of conduct violations and administrative consequences supported these perceptions by showing that the frequency of violations decreased as the school year passed. On the contrary, the researcher found that data on suspension rates showed an increase in the frequency of offenses increased per school year. This conflict between the opinions expressed by the stakeholders and the actual data on student infractions and repeat suspensions led the researcher to the conclusion that the PBS program was not as effective as perceived by the major stakeholders and that further study may be required to determine its effectiveness.

Significance of the Study

The significance of the study will help educators with the understanding of how effective PBS programs can modify problem behaviors in the school setting. This study provided the perceptions of faculty members, parents, and students regarding the PBS program as it was implemented in one school, which helps educators decide whether the PBS program is another behavior intervention program that could help curb problematic student behavior in their respective schools. This study was also beneficial because, despite the positive feedback on PBS programs from previous studies such as Zuma and McDougall (2004), Lassen, Steele and Sailor (2006), and Bohanon et al. (2006), the PBS program, as it was implemented in this particular school, was not as effective as it was in other situations, especially in curbing the number of repeat offenders.

The findings of the study can also be helpful to the administrators of School A in determining which aspects of their program should be improved, and the suggestions provided by the respondents should provide these administrators of an idea where to start improving the program. Lastly, it can also encourage the administrators of School A to explore other options to curb the number of student code of conduct violations.

Limitations

The study was limited in the sense that it used information from only a specific period in time. It analyzed only data from three school years: the year before the program was implemented, the year the program was first implemented, and the year after the program was implemented, which could have limited the study's range and scope. There may be a need to evaluate the program over a longer scope in time in consideration of the fact that it may take some time for the program to integrate itself into the school community and have a measurable effect on the student body. The researcher also considered the small number of participants in the study a limitation. The perceptions of such a small percentage might not reflect the opinion of the school community. The findings of the study regarding the perceptions of the major stakeholders might be considered more valid and reliable if there had been more participants to provide the data to be used for the analysis.

Another major limitation was that the effectiveness of the PBS program was only studied in one school. It might be more useful to compare results from various schools that implemented the PBS program to gauge its effectiveness as opposed to making a conclusion based on the results from just one school. Given more time to research, the researcher would like to compare the overall results of this school's study with another similar school with the same program.

Implications

The implications of this study helped provide an insight into the perceptions of a specific group of faculty members, parents, and students on the PBS program. The findings of this study could be of interest to administrators and teachers who are trying to find a behavior intervention program that will work for their schools. For administrators who also experience problems with student discipline, the results of the study can serve as suggestions on how to modify their respective behavior modification programs for more successful implementation; it could encourage them to seek out alternative discipline programs. For teachers, the comments revealed in the study underscored the importance of consistency in implementing school-wide programs for the benefit of the students. It could also be of interest for parents who want to learn more about the PBS program and how it worked in this particular school. The results of this study revealed that the PBS program did have a positive effect on decreasing the number of behavior referrals but not on curbing the incidences of repeat offenses. These results provided further support for the PBS program as an effective behavior intervention program to augment student discipline programs in various schools. This program can also be used to educate students in environments of deeply rooted societal problems about how to make the proper choices that lead to good consequences. It can also be used for exceptional learners who have a greater need for counseling. The study also opened the doors into further research about the program and its effects on students of different demographic settings such as age and socioeconomic status. Further research studies might also delve into the specific factors that make the PBS program effective in terms of dealing with student misbehavior.

Recommendations

Due to the difficulty of generating large-scale participation for this study, it is recommended that future researchers conduct a study in a school where the major stakeholders are more willing and able to devote time to the study, particularly in a school with which they are acquainted or familiar. Also, given the limitations of the study, it might benefit future researchers if they are able to utilize some of the same survey instruments used in previous studies.

If possible, the next researchers on this topic should try to get a larger sample population, allowing the researchers to give more comprehensive and accurate data regarding the topic. Also, a quantitative study on the effects of the PBS program might be more effective if it was conducted using data from a school that had implemented the program for more than 2 years to allow future researchers to study the effects of the PBS program on a more long-term basis. Researchers can also conduct studies comparing the long-term effects of the PBS program in different schools to determine why it is successful for some schools and not for others as in the case of School A in this study.

Summary

In chapter 5, the researcher discussed the findings of the study analysis and the implications of these results. An overall discussion of the perceptions of major stakeholders on the PBS program regarding the program's implementation and its effectiveness was provided. The researcher also discussed the significance of the study in light of schools that are searching for behavior intervention programs to help decrease their incidences of behavior referrals. The limitations of the study were discussed, and the implications for school administrators and faculty members were provided. Recommendations were made for further studies.

REFERENCES

Achilles, G. M., McLaughlin, M. J., & Croninger, R. G. (2007). Sociocultural correlates of disciplinary exclusion among students with emotional, behavioral, and learning disabilities in the SEELS national dataset. *Journal of Behavioral and Emotional Disorders, 15*(1), 33-45.

American Psychiatric Association. (1994). *Diagnostic and statistical manual of mental disorder* (4ᵗʰ ed.). Washington, DC: Author.

American Psychiatric Association. (2000). *Diagnostic and statistical manual of mental disorders: DSM-IVTR* (4ᵗʰ ed.). Washington, DC: Author.

Anderson, J. C., Williams, S., McGee, R., & Silva, A. (1987). DSM-III disorders in preadolescent children. *Archives of General Psychiatry, 44*, 69-80.

Barrett, S. B., Bradshaw, C. P., & Lewis-Palmer, T. (2008). Maryland statewide PBIS initiative systems, evaluation, and next steps. *Journal of Positive Behavior Interventions, 10*(2), 105-113.

Benedict, E. A., Horner, R. H., & Squires, J. K. (2007). Assessment and implementation of positive behavior support in preschools. *TECSE, 27*(3), 174-192.

Biemer, P. P., & Lieberg, L. (2003). *Introduction to survey quality.* Hoboken, NJ: John Wiley & Sons.

Bohanon, H., Fenning, P., Carney, K. L., Minnis-Kim, M. J., Anderson-Harriss, S.,

Moroz, K. B., et al. (2006). School-wide application of positive behavior support in an urban high school: A case study. *Journal of Positive Behavior Interventions, 8*(3), 131-145.

Carr, E., Dunlap, G., Horner, R. H., Koegel, R. L., Turnbull, A. P., Sailor, W., et al. (2002). Positive behavior support: Evolution of an applied science. *Journal of Positive Behavior Interventions, 4*(1), 4-16.

Cihak, D., Alberto, P. A., & Frederick, L. D. (2007). Use of brief functional analysis and intervention evaluation in public settings. *Journal of Positive Behavior Interventions, 9*(2), 80-93.

Clements, J., & Martin, N. (2002). *Assessing behaviors regarded as problematic for people with developmental disabilities.* London, England: Jessica Kingsley.

Cooper, D. R., & Schindler, P.S. (2003) *Business research and methods* (8th ed.). New York, NY: McGraw-Hill.

Creswell, J. W. (2002). *Research design: Qualitative, quantitative, and mixed-method approaches* (2nd ed.). London, England: Sage.

Delaware Department of Education. (2008). *Delaware education state report card.* Retrieved from http://www.doe.k12.de.us/info/reportcard/de_edreportcard 200607v2.pdf

Downs, A., & Smith, T. (2004). Emotional understanding, cooperation, and social behavior in high-functioning children with autism. *Journal of Autism and Development Disorder, 34,* 625-635.

Eli, I., Baht, R., & Blacher, S. (2004). Prediction of success and failure of behavior modification as treatment for dental anxiety. *Eur J Oral Sci, 112,* 311-315.

Fairbanks, S., Sugai, G., Guardino, D., & Lathrop, M. (in press). An evaluation of a collaborative social behavior response to intervention system of behavior support for second-grade students. *Exceptional Children.*

Feeney, T., & Ylvisaker, M. (2008). Context-sensitive cognitive-behavioral supports for young children with TBI: A second replication study. *Journal of Positive Behavior Interventions, 1*(2), 115-128.

Filter, K. J., McKenna, M. J., Benedict, E. A., Horner, R. H., Todd, A. W., & Watson, J. (2007). Check-in/checkout: A post hoc evaluation of an efficient, secondary- level targeted intervention for reducing problem behaviors in schools. *Education and Treatment of Children, 30,* 69-84.

Flannery, B., & Horner, R. (1994). The relationship between predictability and problem behavior for students with severe disabilities. *Journal of Behavioral Education, 4,* 157-176.

Franzen, K., & Kamps, D. (2008). The utilization and effects of positive behavior support strategies on an urban school playground. *Journal of Positive Behavior Interventions, 10*(3), 150-161.

Fuchs, D., Fuchs, L. S., Mathes, P. G., & Simmons, D. C. (1997). Peer-assisted learning strategies: Making classrooms more responsible to diversity. *American Educational Research Journal, 34*, 174-206.

Goodman, W. K. (1999). Obsessive-compulsive disorder: Diagnosis and treatment. *Journal of Clinical Psychiatry, 60*, 27-32.

Goodwin, F. K., & Jamison, F. R. (1990). *Manic-depressive illness.* New York, NY: Oxford University Press.

Hagekull, B., & Hammarberg, A. (2004). The role of teachers' perceived control and children's characteristics in interactions between 6-year-olds and their teachers. *Scandinavian Journal of Psychology, 45*, 301-312.

Hamilton, C., & Howes, C. E. (1992). Contextual constraints on the concordance of mother-child and teacher-child relationships. In R. Pianta (Ed.), *Beyond the parent: The role of other adults in children's lives* (pp. 41-60). San Francisco, CA: Jossey-Bass.

Hendley, S. L. (2007). Use positive behavior support for inclusion in the general education classroom. *Intervention in School and Clinic, 42*, 225-228.

Horner, R. H., Todd, A. W., Lewis-Palmer, T., Irvin, L. K., Sugai, G., & Boland, B. J. (2004). The school-wide evaluation tool: A research instrument for assessing school-wide positive behavior support. *Journal of Positive Behavior Interventions, 6*(1), 3-12.

Howes, C. (2000). Social-emotional classroom climate in child care, child-teacher relationships, and children's second-grade peer relations. *Social Development, 9*(2), 192-204.

Hyman, S. E., & Rudorfer, M. V. (2000). Depressive and bipolar mood disorders. *American Journal of Psychiatry, 157*, 896-903.

Kamps, D. M., Barbetta, P. M., Leonard, B. R., & Delquadri, J. (1994). Classwide peer tutoring: An integration strategy to improve reading skills and promote peer interactions among students with autism and general education peers. *Journal of Applied Behavior Analysis, 27*, 49-61.

Kashani, J. H., Carlson, G. A., Beck, N. C., Hoeper, E. W., Corcoran, C. M., McAllister, J. A., et al. (1987). Depression, depressive symptoms, and depressed mood among a community sample of adolescents. *American Journal of Psychiatry, 144*, 931-934.

Kashani, J. H., & Orvaschel, H. (1988). Anxiety disorders in mid-adolescence: A community sample. *American Journal of Psychiatry, 145*, 960-964.

Kern, L., & Clemens, L. H. (2007). Antecedent strategies to promote appropriate classroom behavior. *Psychology in the Schools, 44*, 65-75.

Killu, K, Weber, P. K., Derby, M. K., & Baretto, A. (2006). Behavior intervention planning and implementation of positive behavioral support plans: An examination of states' adherence to standards for practice. *Journal of Positive Behavior Interventions, 8*(4), 195-200.

Kincaid, D., Childs, K., Blasé, K. A., & Wallace, F. (2007). Identifying barriers and facilitators in implementing school-wide positive behavior support. *Journal of Positive Behavior Interventions, 9*(3), 174-184.

Koegel, R. L., Koegel, K. L., & Schreibman, L. (1991). Assessing and training parents in teaching pivotal behaviors. In R. J. Prinz (Ed.), *Advances in behavioral assessment of children and families* (pp. 65-82). Greenwich, CT: JAI Press.

Lassen, S. R., Steele, M. M., & Sailor, W. (2006). The relationship of school-wide positive behavior support to academic achievement in an urban middle school. *Psychology in the Schools, 43*, 701-712.

Leonard, H. L., Goldberger, E. L., Rapoport, J. L., Cheslow, D. L., & Swedo, S. E. (1990). Childhood rituals: Normal development or obsessive-compulsive symptoms? *Journal of the American Academy of Child and Adolescent Psychiatry, 29*, 17-23.

Lewis, T., & Sugai, G. (1999). Effective behavior support: A systems approach to proactive school-wide management. *Focus on Exceptional Children, 31*(6), 1-24.

Lovaas, O. I. (1987). Behavioral treatment and normal educational and intellectual functioning in young autistic children. *Journal of Consulting and Clinical Psychology, 55*, 3-9.

Mass-Galloway, R. L., Panyan, M. V., Smith, C. R., & Wessendorf, N. (2008). Systems change with school-wide positive behavior supports: Iowa's work in progress. *Journal of Positive Behavior Interventions, 111*(2), 129-135.

McIntosh, I., Horner, R. H., Chard, D. J., Boland, J. B., & Good R. H., III. (2006). The use of reading and behavior screening measures to predict nonresponse to school- wide positive behavior support: A longitudinal analysis. *School Psychology Review, 35*, 275-291.

Meltzer, H., Gatward, R., Goodman, R., & Ford, T. (2000). *Mental health of children and adolescents in Great Britain.* London, England: The Stationery Office.

Mesibov, G. D., Browder, G. M., & Kirkland, C. (2002). Using individualized schedules as a component of positive behavioral support for students with developmental disabilities. *Journal of Positive Behavior Interventions, 4*(2), 73-79.

Muscott, A. H., Mann, E. L., & LeBrun, L. R. (2008). Positive behavioral interventions and supports in New Hampshire: Effects of large-scale implementation of school- wide positive behavior support on student discipline and academic achievement. *Journal of Positive Behavior Interventions, 10*(3), 190-205.

Obsessive-Compulsive Foundation. (1998). Retrieved from http://www.ocfoundation.org/ocf1010a.htm

Perrin, S., Smith, P., & Yule, W. (2000). Practitioner review: The assessment and treatment of posttraumatic stress disorder in children and adolescents. *Journal of Child Psychology and Psychiatry, 41*, 277-289.

Pianta, R. C., Steinberg, M., & Rollins, K. (1995). The first 2 years of school: Teacher- child relationships and deflections in children's classroom adjustment. *Developmental Psychopathology, 7*, 295-312.

Royal Australian and New Zealand College of Psychiatrists Clinical Practice Guidelines Team for Panic Disorder and Agoraphobia. (2003). Australian and New Zealand clinical practice guidelines for the treatment of panic disorder and agoraphobia. *Australian and New Zealand Journal of Psychiatry, 37*, 641-656.

Rydell, A. M., & Henricsson, L. (2004). Elementary school teachers' strategies to handle externalizing classroom behavior: A study of relations between perceived control, teacher orientation, and strategy preferences. *Scandinavian Journal of Psychology, 45,* 93-102.

Safran, S. P. (2006). Using the effective behavior supports survey to guide development of school-wide positive behavior support. *Journal of Positive Behavior Interventions, 8*(1), 3-9.

Saunders, M., Lewis, P., & Thornhill, A. (2003). *Research methods for business students* (3ʳᵈ ed.). New York, NY: Prentice-Hall.

Scott, T. M. (2007). Issues of personal dignity and social validity in school-wide systems of positive behavior support. *Journal of Positive Behavior Interventions, 9*(2), 102-112.

Sprague, J. R., Sugai, G., Horner, R. H., & Walker, H. M. (1999). Using office discipline referral data to evaluate school-wide discipline and violence prevention interventions. *Oregon School Study Council Bulletin, 42*(2), 39-46.

Stevens, R. J., & Slavin, R. E. (1995a). The cooperative elementary school: Effects on students' achievement, attitudes, and social relations. *American Educational Research Journal, 32,* 321-351.

Stevens, R. J., & Slavin, R. E. (1995b). Effects of a cooperative learning approach in reading and writing on academically handicapped and nonhandicapped students. *The Elementary School Journal, 95,* 241-262.

Stufflebeam, D. L. (1971). The relevance of the CIPP evaluation model for educational accountability. *Journal of Research and Development in Education, 5*(1), 19-25.

Stufflebeam, D. L., McKee, H., & Mc Kee, B. (2003, October). *The CIPP model for evaluation.* Paper presented at the conference of the Oregon Program Evaluators Network, Portland, OR.

Substance Abuse and Mental Health Services Association. (2003). *Children's mental health facts: Children and adolescents with mental, emotional, and behavioral disorders.* Rockville, MD: U.S. Department of Health and Human Services, National Mental Health Information Center.

Sugai, G., & Horner, R. H. (1999). Discipline and behavioral support: Practices, pitfalls, and promises. *Effective School Practices, 17*(4), 10-22.

Sugai, G., Horner, R. H., & Todd, A. W. (2000). *Effective behavioral support survey*. Retrieved from http://www.dpi.state.nc.us/docs/positivebehavior/data/surveys/ebssurvey.pdf

Thyer, B. A. (1993). Childhood onset separation anxiety disorder and adult onset agoraphobia: Review of evidence. In C. G. Last (Ed.), *Anxiety across the lifespan: A developmental perspective* (pp. 128-147). New York, NY: Springer.

Todd, A., Kauffman, A., Meyer, G., & Horner, R. H. (2008). The effects of a targeted intervention to reduce problem behaviors: The check-in checkout program. *Journal of Positive Behavior Interventions, 10*(1), 46-55.

Tynan, W. D. (2003). *Learning disorder: Reading*. Wilmington, DE: Alfred I. DuPont Hospital for Children, Division of Behavioral Health.

Wheldall, K., & Beaman, R. (1998). Disruptive classroom behavior: Separating fact from fantasy. In D. Shorrocks-Taylor (Ed.), *Directions in educational psychology* (pp. 230-243). London, England: Whurr.

Zhang, D., Katsiyannis, A., & Herbst, M. (2004). Disciplinary exclusions in special education: A four-year analysis. *Behavioral Disorders, 29*, 337-347.

Zuna, N., & McDougall, D. (2004). Using positive behavioral support to manage avoidance of academic tasks. *Teaching Exceptional Children, 37*(1), 18-24.

APPENDIX A

Faculty and Staff Survey

Faculty and Staff Survey

Please complete the following questionnaire by rating each statement with a 1, 2, 3, 4, or 5. Please use the spaces at the bottom that is provided for your opinion.

1 = A Agree

2 = TA Tend to Agree

3 = U Uncertain

4 = TD Tend to Disagree

5 = D Disagree

_____ 1. This school needs a behavioral intervention program.

_____ 2. The staff fully supported this program.

_____ 3. There were enough resources to properly implement and maintain this program.

_____ 4. There were enough staff development opportunities for staff to learn how to properly teach this program.

_____ 5. I fully understand all of the goals and objectives of this program.

_____ 6. I have done my part to help this program become successful.

_____ 7. Administrators are always available to help support staff in any way with this program.

_____ 8. This program has been effective in helping reduce the number of student code of conduct infractions.

_____ 9. This program could be more effective if a few changes were made.

_____ 10. This program needs to be completely done away with because it is not at all effective.

Now please take the time to provide feedback on the overall effectiveness of the program. Be sure to include specific examples and evidence to support your opinion. For instance, if you feel the program was/was not effective please state why. Also, include any information about changes (if any) that has to be made.

_____

_____

_____

_____

_____

_____

APPENDIX B

Parent Survey

Appendix B

Partial Survey

Parent Survey

Please complete the following questionnaire by rating each statement with a 1, 2, 3, 4, or 5. Please use the spaces at the bottom that is provided for your opinion.

1 = A Agree

2 = TA Tend to Agree

3 = U Uncertain

4 = TD Tend to Disagree

5 = D Disagree

_____ 1. This school needs a behavioral intervention program.

_____ 2. As a parent I fully support this program.

_____ 3. There were enough resources available to properly inform me of how to support this program at home.

_____ 4. There were enough opportunities for parents to learn about this program.

_____ 5. I fully understand all of the goals and objectives of this program.

_____ 6. I have done my part to help this program become successful.

_____ 7. Administrators are always available to help support parents in any way with this program.

_____ 8. This program has been effective in helping reduce the number of student code of conduct infractions.

_____ 9. This program could be more effective if a few changes were made.

_____ 10. This program needs to be completely done away with because it is not at all effective.

Now please take the time to provide feedback on the overall effectiveness of the program. Be sure to include specific examples and evidence to support your opinion. For instance, if you feel the program was/was not effective please state why. Also, include any information about changes (if any) that has to be made.

_____

_____

_____

_____

_____

_____

APPENDIX C

Student Survey

Student Survey

Please complete the following questionnaire by rating each statement with a 1, 2, 3, 4, or 5. Please use the spaces at the bottom that is provided for your opinion.

1 = A Agree

2 = TA Tend to Agree

3 = U Uncertain

4 = TD Tend to Disagree

5 = D Disagree

_____ 1. This school needs a behavioral intervention program.

_____ 2. The students fully supported this program.

_____ 3. There were enough resources to properly teach the lessons in this program.

_____ 4. There were enough opportunities for students to use the skills they learned.

_____ 5. I fully understand all of the goals and objectives of this program.

_____ 6. I have done my part to help this program become successful.

_____ 7. Administrators are always available to help support students in any way with this program.

_____ 8. This program has been effective in helping reduce the number of student code of conduct infractions.

_____ 9. This program could be more effective if a few changes were made.

_____ 10. This program needs to be completely done away with because it is not at all effective.

Now please take the time to provide feedback on the overall effectiveness of the program. Be sure to include specific examples and evidence to support your opinion. For instance, if you feel the program was/was not effective please state why. Also, include any information about changes (if any) that has to be made.

_____

_____

_____

_____

_____

_____

ABOUT THE AUTHOR

Dr.James A. Bracy, a native of Philadelphia, Pennsylvania; my entire educational learning process and endeavors spent in the public-school districts. As a young man with several learning disabilities during my early elementary and middle school matriculation, I would contently find myself off task during academic's activities. While being off task in a classroom environment, this would cause a disturbance around other students who were working on their assignments. The ultimate end to this sad performance was either get put out of the classroom or escorted to the principal's office.

One day in an elementary classroom setting, I am returning to school after the Thanksgiving break. My teacher set alongside me in class. My teacher said, James, if you stay on task today, I have a reward for you, but if you get off task, you cannot receive it. Yes, I stay on task all that day completing the academic seat work and looking at the clock. You're right; I did earn the reward. You see, my teacher's Positive Behavior Support Program not only helped me but also with other students that were in that classroom on a smaller scale. You can imagine how significant this Positive Behavior Support Program can be beneficial for teachers and students.

Dr. James A. Bracy
Educational Achievements
PALMER THEOLOGICAL SIEMINARY
Master of Divinity (MDiv.)
2013-2017
NOVA SOUTHEASTERN UNIVERSITY
Doctor of Education Educational Leadership
205-2011
DELAWARE STATE UNIVERSITY
Master of Art Degree in Curriculum and Instruction
1998-2000
DELAWARE STATE UNIVERSITY
Bachelor of Art Degree in Special Education Elementary Education
Minor - Elementary Education & Secondary Teaching
1987-1991
Standard Certification, Principal / Assistant of Elementary School
Standard Certification, Principal / Assistant of Secondary School
Standard Certification, Teacher of Exceptional Children – LD, SED, MH
(1-12)
Professional Status, Elementary Teacher (1-8)
2012-2018
CHRISTAIN INTERNATIONAL COLLEGE
Associate's degree,
Theology/Theological Studies
1982-1984
SPIRIT & LIFE BIBLE COLLEGE
Associate's degree
Religious Education
1982-1984

Printed in the United States
By Bookmasters

Printed in the United States
By Bookmasters